851.1
D192izce

NF
8.99
NoBind

FACES FROM
DANTE'S *INFERNO*

D1105965

DISCARD

FACES FROM
DANTE'S *INFERNO*

Who They Are, What They Say, And What It All Means

PETER CELANO

With quotations from Inferno *translated by*
Henry Wadsworth Longfellow (1807–1884)

And illustrations by
Gustave Doré (1832–1883)

PARACLETE PRESS
BREWSTER, MASSACHUSETTS

2013 First Printing

Faces from Dante's Inferno: *Who they are, what they say, and what it all means*

Copyright © 2013 by Paraclete Press, Inc.

ISBN: 978-1-61261-421-2

Henry Wadsworth Longfellow's translation of *The Divine Comedy* is in the public domain, as are the illustrations by the great Gustave Doré.

All quotations from the Holy Scriptures are from the New Revised Standard Version Bible, copyright 1989, Division of Christian Education of the National Council of the Churches of Christ in the United States of America. Used by permission. All rights reserved.

The Paraclete Press name and logo (dove on cross) are trademarks of Paraclete Press, Inc.

Library of Congress Cataloging-in-Publication Data:
Celano, Peter.
  Faces from Dante's Inferno : who they are, what they say, and what it all means / Peter Celano ; with quotations from Inferno translated by Henry Wadsworth Longfellow (1807-1884) and illustrations by Gustave Doré (1832-1883).
     pages cm
  ISBN 978-1-61261-421-2 (trade pbk.)
  1. Dante Alighieri, 1265-1321. Inferno. I. Title.
  PQ4443.C43 2013
  851'.1—dc23   2013016554

10 9 8 7 6 5 4 3 2 1

All rights reserved. No portion of this book may be reproduced, stored in an electronic retrieval system, or transmitted in any form or by any means—electronic, mechanical, photocopy, recording, or any other—except for brief quotations in printed reviews, without the prior permission of the publisher.

Published by Paraclete Press
Brewster, Massachusetts
www.paracletepress.com

Printed in the United States of America

CONTENTS

TIMELINE

Dante's Real Life

Spring **1265**	Born in Florence
1283	Both of Dante's parents are dead before he turns 18
1285	He marries Gemma Donati
1287	His first child, a son, is born, while he's busy writing the lyric love poems to Beatrice in his first book, *Vita Nuova* ("New Life")
1291–94	Dante studies with the Dominicans and Franciscans in Florence
1295	His political career begins
June **1300**	Elected one of the six priors (highest office) in Florence
Jan. **1302**	Banished from Florence for two years by his political enemies
March **1302**	Sentence increased to death, should he ever attempt to return
1312–18	Living in Verona, where he finishes the *Comedy*
1318–21	Living in Ravenna
Sept. **1321**	Death from malaria, age 56

Dante's Imaginative Life

1274	At nine, Dante falls in love with Beatrice "upon first sight"
June **1290**	Beatrice dies, but takes on a new life in Dante's imagination
1300	"Midway upon the journey of our life," the *Divine Comedy* begins, during Holy Week, in the year 1300

The World at Large

1291	Acre, the last Christian Crusader stronghold in the Holy Land, falls to Muslim forces
1294	The brief, disastrous papacy of Celestine V, followed by the election of Pope Boniface VIII
1300	Boniface VIII declares the first "Year of Jubilee," entitling every pilgrim to indulgences for visiting the sacred sites of Rome
1303	Death of Boniface VIII
1305	French Pope Clement V is elected, and the papacy leaves Italy, relocating to Avignon, France, beginning the "Babylonian Captivity" of the Church

FACES FROM
DANTE'S *INFERNO*

INTRODUCTION

A PORTRAIT OF DANTE ALIGHIERI

HE GREAT POET WE ALL KNOW SIMPLY as "Dante" was born in Florence, Italy, most likely in 1265. Experts have settled on that year largely because of what Dante says at the beginning of the *Inferno*:

Midway upon the journey of our life
   I found myself within a forest dark,
   For the straightforward pathway had been lost.
      (I, lines 1–3)

Everyone in Dante's day used a phrase from the Bible, Psalm 90 (or Psalm 89, as they were numbered in the medieval Latin Vulgate), to understand that the average life span of a human being was 70 years.

"Threescore and ten," it still reads in the Douay-Rheims translation. So it is fairly safe to assume that Dante was 35 years old when the fictional events of the *Inferno* open, in the year 1300.

His full name was Durante degli Alighieri.

By most accounts, he is to be considered the narrator and subject of his *Divine Comedy*. He is the hero of his own poem, although it has become common to refer to this main character, the narrator who follows Virgil through every stage of hell, discovering and recording all of its atrocities, as simply the "pilgrim."

Dante was brought up in a well-to-do family, educated at fine schools, and taught to recite great poetry from an early age. His family was also proudly Roman, and was often engulfed in the difficult political climate of those days in Florence. Dante would become a victim of these political alliances, himself, in his thirties.

After briefly ruling as one of the six priors (the highest political office) of Florence, Dante was not only ousted from office but also forced into exile when his party, the White Guelphs, was overtaken by the

Black Guelphs. Interestingly, Dante and his political colleagues had the backing of the Holy Roman Emperor, while the opposition was backed by Pope Boniface VIII.

He had a strongly romantic bent about him. We see this most of all in his profound attachment to a young woman by the name of Beatrice. Dante first saw her at the age of nine, and in *Vita Nuova* (New Life), an earlier poem written entirely about Beatrice, Dante muses that it was love at first sight, as well as the most important event of his life.

Beatrice was actually Beatrice Portinari, an otherwise obscure figure in history whom Dante nevertheless immortalized in his writings. In real life, they hardly knew each other. If they had lived in modern times, we might say they never even went on a date together. But the thirteenth and fourteenth centuries were the era of courtly love poetry, and Dante was a master of the form. After Beatrice died in 1290, surely never having had any sort of real relationship with the young Dante (she married someone else—a banker), and despite the fact that Dante married another woman, who bore him children, Dante devoted his life's work to Beatrice. In the *Divine Comedy*, she is the most important character, after the pilgrim/narrator/Dante himself, and Virgil.

Beatrice's presence is mostly felt in the portions of Dante's masterpiece that come after the *Inferno*—beyond what this present book is about. It is, according to the poet's imagining, Beatrice who, toward the end of Book Two, *Purgatorio*, picks up from Virgil the task of guiding the pilgrim who has seen hell and purgatory, even calling Dante by name (canto XXX, 55). And then she guides him toward the beatific vision of God in *Paradiso*, or paradise.

CHAPTER ONE

What Is the *Inferno?*

HERE ARE THREE PARTS, OR BOOKS, to Dante's *Divine Comedy*. Each contains thirty-three cantos, or chapters:

Inferno (Hell)
Purgatorio (Purgatory), and
Paradiso (Paradise, or Heaven)

So as you can see, the book you are holding only deals with the first third of Dante's masterpiece. But it is this first third that has always captured the human imagination.

Dante began writing the complete work, which he called simply his *Commedia* (The Comedy) in about 1300. It was the famous and more bawdy poet of

Fun facts about Dante's *Divine Comedy*

The magical number 9

Dante wrote of hell with 9 circles, Mount Purgatory with 9 rings, and then there are 9 celestial bodies in paradise.

Stars, stars, stars

Dante concludes each part—*Inferno, Purgatorio*, and *Paradiso*—with the word "stars" (*stelle*, in Italian).

O the Vulgarity!

Many of Dante's contemporaries found it shocking that he would write of sin and redemption in so "vulgar" a language as Italian.

the following generation, Boccaccio, who added the adjective *Divina* (Divine) to the title, effectively dubbing it *The Divine Comedy* for all time.

He wrote in verse, although many translations of the work render that verse into prose.

Dante is considered the master of vernacular Italian, and the *Divine Comedy* is generally regarded as the greatest work of Italian literature. The Italian language was still in its infancy as a literary language in Dante's time. Most serious writings were still being composed in Latin.

Up until Dante's time, there had been very little written about hell. The Bible barely mentions it. Clergy were known to preach of hell's existence, reminding their listeners that death was inevitable, and that the afterlife was real. But no writer had ever taken on the subject for a full-length, reflective work, before Dante.

Nevertheless, Dante draws on many classic sources in writing this poem. Virgil's *Aeneid* is probably the most obvious, but Dante also included

Ovid and other sources of Greek mythology. Dante was inspired, also, by Augustine's *Confessions*. And there are many references to Holy Scripture in these poetic verses—particularly the Psalms, the prophets, the Gospels, and Revelation.

Of course, the way in which Dante writes about hell is entirely fictional. The technical term for it is not actually "fiction," but "allegory." What exactly is an allegory?

An allegory is a fiction that aims to communicate truths about a situation using symbolic language and referents. Most of its action takes place internally, within the thoughts and feelings of a central character—in this case, Dante himself. In other words, action, plot, and setting that are presented as fictitious are still intended to communicate something very true about life. There are other classic allegories in Christian literature, such as John Bunyan's *Pilgrim's Progress*.

The journey of Dante and Virgil begins on hell's outskirts on the evening before Good Friday, in the year 1300, as they slowly make their way down through each of hell's nine circles. In circle one, the pilgrim Dante discovers what are often called "virtuous pagans," those who lived exemplary lives, but before or without the light of Christ (see chapter 5).

Then, beginning in circle two (chapter 6 and after), the lower and lower places of hell are increasingly severe. The punishments of sinners became more and more horrific.

The early circles of hell are where we see those who committed sins such as lust, gluttony, and wrath—sins that come most naturally to the human person, but that we nevertheless are supposed to avoid with God's help.

By circle seven we find those who have been violent to themselves, to their neighbors, and toward God.

Circle eight reveals panderers, hypocrites, thieves, seducers, and others who have committed sins that involve purpose and plotting.

And in the lowest circle of all are found what Dante calls the treacherous, the malicious, the traitors.

The central message of the *Inferno* is the reality and realization of sin. The pilgrim begins "within a forest dark," or a "dark wood," in other translations. This darkness is meant as sin. And as he tells his story of walking through hell, he is slowly and dramatically transformed, discovering the power of sin in a human life. By the end of the poem—when he sees Satan face to face—he already knows more about darkness and sin than any person should.

Peter S. Hawkins, a professor of religion and literature at Yale, describes the *Inferno* this way. It is a picture of

> [O]ur world without grace, our cities without love, our will to power without mercy. In hell, the self is sovereign, cut off, frozen in obsession and monomania, always alone no matter how dense the crowd. The journey through *Inferno* also

engages Dante's empathy by reminding him how often evil is a mystery of flawed goodness. [And] by the time he comes into the grotesque presence of Satan, hell has been exposed for what it is—a world where earth's atrocities rage unchecked for all eternity.[1]

The Darkening Sky of the First Night

CHAPTER TWO

THE FIRST THREE FACES
Virgil, Aeneas, and
St. Paul

cantos I and II

HESE ARE CHARACTERS WHOM WE meet in the Dark Wood before the journey into hell begins. They help to explain the purpose of the journey that Dante, and every reader of the *Inferno*, is about to take.

Virgil

- First appears in canto I when Dante is wandering lost in a wilderness, pursued by a leopard and then a wolf.

- The greatest of the ancient Roman poets.

- Lived before the time of Christ; was, therefore, a "pagan" poet.

- Ironically, Virgil's soul is itself located in hell, according to Dante, even though he is the narrator's tour guide through that place of eternal suffering.

Dante's first words to Virgil:

> "Have pity on me . . .
> Whiche'er thou art, or shade or real man!"
> (I, 65–66)

clearly echo the opening of Psalm 51. Then, Dante says:

> "Now, art thou that Virgilius and that fountain
> Which spreads abroad so wide a river of
>   speech?"
> (I, 79–80)

In other words, "Aren't you that great poet, Virgil, whose words are powerful like a mighty river?"

Dante goes on, saying also to Virgil:

> "O, of the other poets honor and light,
> Avail me the long study and great love
> That have impelled me to explore thy volume!
> Thou art my master, and my author thou."
> (I, 82–85)

In other words, "You are the best poet of them all, my teacher, and the one who can best tell me what to do and where to go from here."

And so, Virgil guides good Dante out of the dark wood. He will be the poet's tour guide through hell.

As Virgil explains:

> "Therefore I think and judge it for thy best
> Thou follow me, and I will be thy guide,
> And lead thee hence through the eternal
> place,
> Where thou shalt hear the desperate
> lamentations,

Shalt see the ancient spirits disconsolate,

Who cry out each one for the second death."
(I, 112–117)

Aeneas

- First appears in canto II, not in bodily form, but in the imagination of Dante, who recalls how Virgil wrote powerfully of the earlier, famous traveler.

- Aeneas is the hero of Virgil's poem *The Aeneid*.

- *The Aeneid* recounts Aeneas's journey from the Battle of Troy to the land of Italy, becoming the ancient founder and "father" of Rome.

- Aeneas is a symbol of what Dante considers to be Rome's divinely ordained role in human history, for Aeneas's Rome became the cradle for all civilization, and the church.

The figure of Aeneas was a connection between Dante's ever-present political and religious views. In a treatise written simultaneously with the *Inferno*, Dante made the following argument, which sounds shockingly wrong to our twenty-first-century ears:

> I therefore affirm that it was by right, and not by usurping, that the Roman people took on the office of the monarch (which is called "empire") over all men. This can be proved firstly as follows: it is appropriate that the noblest race should rule over all the others; the Roman people was the noblest; therefore it was appropriate that they should rule over all the others.

Back at the beginning of the journey into hell, speaking to Virgil, Dante compares himself unfavorably to Aeneas:

. . . "Poet, who guidest me,

Regard my manhood, if it be sufficient,

Ere to the arduous pass thou dost confide me.

I not Aeneas am . . .

Nor I, nor others, think me worthy of it."
(II, 10–12, 32–33)

But Dante places himself in Virgil's hands.

St. Paul

- First appears in canto II, referred to as "the Chosen Vessel" of God.

- The New Testament identifies Paul as the first apostle of Christ to take the gospel to the Gentiles.

- He was raised a Jew, persecuted Christians for a time, and then had a conversion experience on the road to Damascus that changed his life, and the life of the church, forever.

Feeling unworthy of the journey Virgil is taking him upon, Dante first compared himself to Aeneas, and now compares himself unworthily to St. Paul:

> "Thither went afterwards the Chosen Vessel,
> To bring back comfort thence unto that Faith,
> Which of salvation's way is the beginning.
> But I, why thither come, or who concedes it?"
> (II, 28–31)

Aeneas was the founder of holy Rome, while St. Paul is recognized as specially appointed by God to show the world the way of salvation.

Virgil reassures Dante, saying:

> "If I have well thy language understood . . .
> Thy soul attainted is with cowardice,
> Which many times a man encumbers so,
> It turns him back from honored enterprise. . . ."
> (II, 43, 45–47)

Because, as Virgil explains to Dante, he has seen a vision of a certain lady who has assured him that, with Virgil's help, Dante will find his way.

CHAPTER THREE

HIS BELOVED LADY
Beatrice

canto II

Beatrice

- A character based upon a girl Dante knew in childhood.

- First appears in canto II, in the descriptive words of Virgil: "a fair, saintly Lady."

- Appears by name later in canto II, speaking to Virgil: "Beatrice am I, who do bid thee go."

- We're told that she has already glimpsed God in heaven, but left glory long enough to instruct Virgil to look after Dante on this otherworldly journey.

- Dante first wrote about Beatrice, his love for her, and his belief that romantic love prepares a person for divine love, in a poem titled *Vita Nuova* (New Life).

 IKE ST. PAUL, BEATRICE CLAIMS TO HAVE been granted a vision of heaven. St. Paul wrote of such an experience in 2 Corinthians 12:2-4:

I know a person in Christ who fourteen years ago was caught up to the third heaven—whether in the body or out of the body I do not know; God knows. And I know that such a person—whether in the body or out of the body I do not know; God knows—was caught up into Paradise and heard things that are not to be told, that no mortal is permitted to repeat.

And now, Beatrice tells Virgil that she has come from heaven to the outskirts of hell, looking for Virgil, so concerned she was about Dante:

> A friend of mine, and not the friend of fortune,
>> Upon the desert slope is so impeded
>> Upon his way, that he has turned through
>>> terror,
> And may, I fear, already be so lost,
>> That I too late have risen to his succour,
>> From that which I have heard of him in
>>> Heaven.
> Bestir thee now, and with thy speech ornate,
>> And with what needful is for his release,
>> Assist him so, that I may be consoled.
> Beatrice am I, who do bid thee go;
>> I come from there, where I would fain return;
>> Love moved me, which compelleth me to speak.
>> (II, 61–72)

She goes on to say that the Virgin Mary herself is grieving at what stands in Dante's way. St. Lucy, also, she says, is advocating for Dante from heaven. Together, three great women are in heaven cheering Dante on.

Virgil acts on the words of Beatrice, turning to Dante and saying, "unto thee I came, as she desired" (II, 118). And so Dante follows Virgil once and for all, turning to us at the conclusion of canto II to say ". . . and when he had moved, / I entered on the deep and savage way" (II, 141–42).

He is now prepared to enter the gates of hell.

Beatrice Pointing the Way

The Gates of Hell

CHAPTER FOUR

JUST OUTSIDE HELL'S GATES
Pope Celestine V

canto III

UST OUTSIDE OF HELL'S GATES are many nameless souls sobbing and sighing, whose lives, according to canto III, were either apathetic, contemptible, or without honor.

Pope Celestine V

- The first person to be recognized by Dante at hell's gates is Celestine V.

- Celestine V spent most of his first 80 years living as a Benedictine hermit in the mountains northeast of Rome.

- His name was Brother Peter Morrone.

- Morrone was surprisingly elected pope in 1294, ruled briefly as Celestine V, and resigned the Chair of St. Peter before Christmas that same year.

- He was the first pope in history to willingly, and on his own accord, resign the holy office.

Dante does not name Celestine V by name. Doing so would be to give too much honor to someone that he believed was so cowardly. Dante narrates:

> When some among them I had recognized,
> I looked, and I beheld the shade of him
> Who made through cowardice the great refusal.
> (III, 58–60)

But most of all, Dante despised Celestine's successor Boniface VIII, whose papacy was made possible by Celestine's abdication. The lines then used by the poet to describe Celestine, and those like him, outside hell's gates, show how judgmental Dante could be:

> Forthwith I comprehended, and was certain,
>> That this the sect was . . .
>> Hateful to God and to his enemies.
> These miscreants, who never were alive,
>> Were naked, and were stung exceedingly
>> By gadflies and by hornets that were there.
>> (III, 61–66)

Despite Dante's condemning of the one "Who made through cowardice the great refusal," the Catholic Church made Celestine V a saint soon after his death.

The First Circle of Hell

CHAPTER FIVE

CIRCLE ONE
Ovid, Electra, Plato, Galen, Saladin, and Averroes

canto II

N THIS FIRST CIRCLE OF HELL, DANTE and Virgil enter and see patriarchs and other famous figures from the Old Testament who were saved by Christ after the Crucifixion, when he descended into hell to raise up those who knew the truth of Christ before his advent. This event is not told in Scripture itself, but is resident in the line from the Apostle's Creed that refers to Christ who "descended into hell." The event is known to Christian tradition as the "Harrowing of Hell."

Abel, Noah, Moses, Abraham, Jacob, Rachel, and David are mentioned by name. "[Christ] made them blessed," Virgil explains, followed by:

> And thou must know, that earlier than these
> Never were any human spirits saved.
> (IV, 61–63)

Then, their attention turns to others who lived before the Christian era. As Virgil explains:

> That they sinned not; and if they merit had,
>   'Tis not enough, because they had not baptism,
>   Which is the portal of the Faith thou holdest;
> And if they were before Christianity,
>   In the right manner they adored not God;
>   And among such as these am I myself.
> (IV, 34–39)

Yes, Virgil himself is among these righteous pagans, who, despite their apparent goodness, are in hell without Christ. Then Dante recognizes others:

Ovid

- Another great poet—perhaps the world's most important, other than Homer and Virgil, before Dante.

- He lived and wrote in the decades just before the time of Christ, 43 BC–AD 17/18.

- Author of *Metamorphoses*, a work that retells the world's myths of creation and gods, such as Amor, the Roman god of love (a frequent subject in Dante's other writings).

Electra

- The daughter of Atlas, one of the legendary figures of Troy, as told in Virgil's *Aeneid*.

- Electra is considered one of the "seven heavenly sisters," or the Pleiades sisters, who were turned into stars after their father, Atlas, was forced to carry the heavens on his shoulders.

- According to Greek mythology, Electra was raped by Zeus and gave birth to Dardanus, the founder of Troy.

Plato

- Together with Aristotle, Socrates, Heraclitus, and others, Plato is a philosopher who displayed great knowledge, but apart from God.

- Plato lived from about 424/423–348/347 BC in Greece.

- Plato's philosophy was incorporated into early Christian thought by theologians such as St. Augustine, author of *The City of God*.

There are many others besides, born after the time of Christ, but still who died without Christian baptism:

Galen

- Like Hippocrates (also mentioned), Galen was one of the ancient founders of what became modern medicine.

- A physician who lived AD 129–ca. 200, a proud citizen of the Roman Empire.

- Famous for his studies in anatomy, physiology, and surgery.

Saladin

- Mentioned by Dante after other famous military leaders (such as Brutus) are spotted, "And saw alone, apart, the Saladin." (IV, 129)

- Lived 1137 / 1138–1193, the first Sultan of Egypt and Syria.

- A Muslim (although not mentioned as such in *Inferno*) who led Muslim forces

against European crusaders during the
Third Crusade.

Averroes

- A Spanish Muslim philosopher, whose
  translations introduced Aristotle to
  Christian theologians of both East and
  West.

- Lived 1126–1198.

- Mentioned together with another
  Muslim philosopher, Avicenna, together
  with Saladin and Averroes, making three
  Muslims in otherwise distinguished
  "pagan" company.

CHAPTER SIX

CIRCLE TWO
Minos, Semiramis, Cleopatra, Achilles, Francesca

canto V

ANTE BEGINS CANTO V BY RELATING:

Thus I descended out of the first circle
　Down to the second, that less space begirds,
　And so much greater dole, that goads to wailing.
(V, 1–3)

In other words, "From circle one I went down to the second, narrower than the first, which makes it even more awful with suffering." It is here in this circle of hell that Dante begins to feel more than just sorrowful for the lost, but personally pained by the sight of it all:

> And now begin the dolesome notes to grow
>   Audible unto me; now am I come
>   There where much lamentation strikes upon me.
> (V, 25–27)

In this part of hell, we see those souls who were most wanton in their sinfulness.

Minos

- A son of Zeus, in Greek mythology.

- Famous for sending young children to be devoured by a Minotaur.

- In the *Aeneid,* Virgil describes Minos as a judge of souls in Hades.

Minos

- Serves as a symbol of the fearsome, awful characters, real and imagined, that exist in the darkness of Dante's hell.

Dante writes:

There standeth Minos horribly, and snarls; . . .
Always before him many of them stand;
    They go by turns each one unto the judgment;
    They speak, and hear, and then are downward
        hurled.
(V, 4, 13–15)

Semiramis

- The Greek name of a historical, ancient Assyrian queen from the ninth century BC.

- Many legends were believed about her, according to the ancient world (including by St. Augustine of Hippo).

- Believed to be the widow of King Ninus, the presumed founder of the Babylonian Empire.

- She was believed to have committed incest with her son, who followed his father as king.

Cleopatra

- Lived ca. 69–30 BC.

- The last pharaoh of ancient Egypt.

- Married first to her two brothers, then to Mark Antony. Also had a liaison with

Julius Caesar in order to consolidate her power.

- Dante calls her "Cleopatra the voluptuous" and "she who killed herself for love." (V, 63, 61)

- She is usually depicted as killing herself by enticing a poisonous asp to bite her breast.

Achilles

- Continuing in this circle of hell, populated with the lustful, Dante finds the famous Greek warrior from Homer's *Iliad*, Achilles.

- A mythological figure, one of the Greek demigods.

- Famous for his wrath during the Trojan War, but also for his lust.

- He turned traitor when he saw the Trojan princess Polyxena, seeking to marry her, only to fall victim to an arrow at that moment.

Francesca

- A figure from Italian politics in Dante's day.

- A member of one of the famous ruling families of Florentine politics and society: the Riminis.

- Francesca da Rimini had an affair with her husband's brother, Paolo. Her husband killed them both.

- She speaks to Dante as he passes by, ". . . There is no greater sorrow / Than to be mindful of the happy time / In misery. . . ."
  (V, 121–123)

CHAPTER SEVEN

CIRCLE THREE
Cerberus, Ciacco, Farinata and Tegghiaio, Plutus

canto VI

FTER THE CIRCLE OF HELL WITH
the lustful, we now enter one with the
gluttonous. Dante writes:

New torments I behold, and new tormented
　　Around me, whichsoever way I move,
　　And whichsoever way I turn, and gaze.
(VI, 4–6)

The notion of "seven deadly sins" was already popular and common in Dante's day. These famous seven are lust, gluttony, greed, sloth, pride, envy, and wrath, all of which figure prominently in this first half of the *Inferno*. Medieval Catholic theologians believed that it was these sins that give rise to all the others.

Cerberus

Here, Virgil and Dante come face to face with Cerberus, the three-headed dog of ancient Greek and Roman mythology who guards the gates of the underworld so that all who have entered have no way of escaping.

- Virgil throws fists full of dirt in the dog's mouths.

- Dante compares the beast to a demon, ". . . who so thunders / Over the souls that they would fain be deaf." (VI, 32–33)

Then, one figure is seen sitting upright as Dante and Virgil pass by. It is—

Ciacco

- He speaks to the pair, saying,
  "O thou that art conducted through this Hell,
  . . . recall me, if thou canst."
  (VI, 40–41)

- No one knows for certain whom this figure represented for Dante, or in history.

- But he speaks prophetically about the political turmoil that was well known to Dante in Florence, and he characterizes it all in these sad lines:

  "Envy and Arrogance and Avarice
  Are the three sparks that have all hearts
    enkindled."
  (VI, 74–75)

Farinata and Tegghiaio

- These are names of key political figures in Florence in Dante's day, men ". . . once so worthy," they are mentioned among "others who on good deeds set their thoughts."
(VI, 79)

- "Say where they are, and cause that I may know them;

  For great desire constraineth me to learn

  If Heaven doth sweeten them, or Hell envenom," asks Dante of Virgil.
(VI, 82–84)

- Farinata appears again in canto X; a politician who died in 1264, he was a known heretic in Dante's time.

- Tegghiaio appears again in canto XVI, but we are not told of the sin that landed him in hell.

Plutus

- Then, in the final line of canto VI, Dante glimpses our next character: "There we found Plutus the great enemy."

- Plutus (or "Pluto," in the Latin) was the god of the underworld in ancient Greek mythology. In fact, his original name was not Plutus, but Hades.

- He was also the god of wealth, and therefore a prime symbol of gluttony in every respect.

It is Plutus who is speaking some sort of nonsense to Dante and Virgil, as the following canto opens, and as they wind their way from the third circle of hell to the fourth. He is calling out to "Pape Satan," presumably with the idea that the pope of the underworld is Satan himself. (VII, 1)

Entrance to The Fourth Circle of Hell

CHAPTER EIGHT

CIRCLE FOUR
Monks, Popes, Cardinals, the Angry, the Lazy

canto VII

HERE ARE LONG PORTIONS OF DANTE'S *Inferno* in which no specific historical persons, or even mythic personalities, are mentioned. Instead, we see *categories* of people, resident in one of the circles of hell.

Canto VII is one such portion. No specific characters or examples are mentioned. Instead, broad categories are used to characterize the stingy, the wrathful, and the lazy, as they descend "into the fourth chasm" (VII, 16).

Dante's judgments turn against the signal leaders of the Church.

He describes Monks, Popes, and Cardinals as those:

> In whom doth avarice practice its excess.
> (VII, 48)

Then, as usual, Dante claims to recognize a few specific ones; and Virgil adds that they all lived an "undiscerning life which made them sordid" (VII, 53).

The two men then cross over to the opposite bank of the fourth circle of hell, where they find even greater woe, and people who are forever stuck in the mud of a lagoon, tearing each other apart:

> All of them naked and with angry look.
> (VII, 111)

The Angry

These are not ones who merely felt anger, but ones who gave in to it.

> They smote each other not alone with hands,
>> But with the head and with the breast and feet,
>> Tearing each other piecemeal with their teeth.

Beside them are other people also "fixed in the mire."
(VII, 112–114, 121)

The Lazy

These are those who, despite the beautiful sky and gladdening sun, bear about themselves a ". . . sluggish reek."
(VII, 123)

"Now we are sullen in this sable mire," they look to Dante and explain.
(VII, 124)

Entrance to The Fourth Circle of Hell

In all of these cases, we are faced with Dante's presentation of the pains of hell as a sort of logic that is related somehow directly to true justice. How do we reconcile this?

Justice of God, ah! who heaps up so many
    New toils and sufferings as I beheld?
    And why doth our transgression waste us so?
(VII, 19–21)

Crossing the River Styx

CHAPTER NINE

CIRCLE FIVE
Phlegyas, Filippo Argenti, the Rebellious Angels

canto VIII

HIS IS THE CANTO OF THE *INFERNO* where Dante and Virgil travel across the infamous River Styx, which, according to myth and legend, forms the borderline between earth and Hades. The first face in hell's fifth circle they met is their ferryboat captain, Phlegyas.

Phlegyas

- Appears also in Virgil's *Aeneid* (book VI) as a resident of the underworld, warning others that they should have listened to the gods.

- Here, he shouts to Dante and Virgil, "Now art thou arrived, fell soul?"

- They assure him (and themselves!):

"Phlegyas . . . thou criest out in vain
   For this once . . . thou shalt not have us
   Longer than in the passing of the slough."
(VIII, 18–21)

It is here that the pair meet those who have deliberately turned away from God.

Filippo Argenti

- Another Florentine politician, known to Dante, and active in Dante's day.

- Born into a wealthy family, and known for his infamous anger, often turned upon his enemies.

- Filippo's anger almost seems to border
  on self-hatred, once he's in hell, as
  Dante narrates:

". . . that exasperate spirit Florentine
Turned round upon himself with his own
    teeth."
(VIII, 62-63)

The Rebellious Angels

Midway through canto VIII, we read of this scene
and this question:

More than a thousand at the gates I saw
    Out of the Heavens rained down, who angrily
    Were saying, "Who is this that without death
Goes through the kingdom of the people dead?"
    (VIII, 82–85)

These infamous thousand-plus were believed to be
none other than the rebellious angels who were cast
out of heaven.

More Than a Thousand At The Gate

The Rebellious Angels

- The story of Lucifer's rebellion originated with the ancient Christian theologian Origen.

- Origen thought that the "morning star" of Isaiah 14:1–17 referred to Lucifer.

- Jesus's teaching also contributed to this idea that an angel or angels may have been tossed from heaven.

- Jesus told a crowd in Luke 10:18: "I watched Satan fall from heaven like a flash of lightning."

- The only other biblical text for a story of rebellious and fallen angels appears in Revelation 12:7–14.

- Some ancient commentators also proposed the idea that the "sons of God" mentioned twice in Genesis 6:1–4 are references to angels who turned away from God.

Is the dragon of Revelation 12:7–14 Lucifer?

And war broke out in heaven; Michael and his angels fought against the dragon. The dragon and his angels fought back, but they were defeated, and there was no longer any place for them in heaven. The great dragon was thrown down, that ancient serpent, who is called the Devil and Satan, the deceiver of the whole world—he was thrown down to the earth, and his angels were thrown down with him.

Then I heard a loud voice in heaven, proclaiming,
"Now have come the salvation and the power
    and the kingdom of our God
    and the authority of his Messiah,
for the accuser of our comrades has been thrown down,
    who accuses them day and night before our God.

But they have conquered him by the blood of the Lamb

    and by the word of their testimony,

for they did not cling to life even in the face of death.

Rejoice then, you heavens

    and those who dwell in them!

But woe to the earth and the sea,

    for the devil has come down to you

with great wrath,

      because he knows that his time is short!"

So when the dragon saw that he had been thrown down to the earth, he pursued the woman who had given birth to the male child. But the woman was given the two wings of the great eagle, so that she could fly from the serpent into the wilderness, to her place where she is nourished for a time, and times, and half a time.

The Heretics

CHAPTER TEN

CIRCLE SIX
The Furies, the Heretics, Epicurus

canto IX–X

T THIS POINT, ACCORDING TO DANTE, one of the great divides in hell has been crossed: the City of Dis—a legendary residence (which also figures in Virgil's *Aeneid*) for those thousand or more rebellious angels. What follows next, in the sixth circle of hell, after a few more mythological characters, are the heretics: more who willfully turned against God.

First are

The Furies

- The goddesses of vengeance.

- Figure prominently in Greek mythology, for instance, in Aeschylus's *Oresteia* trilogy of tragic plays.

- Make their residence in the underworld but appear on earth from time to time to torment the living.

"Each one her breast was rending with her nails;
    They beat them with their palms, and cried so
      loud,
    That I for dread pressed close unto the Poet,"
writes Dante.
    (IX, 49–51)

The Heretics

Dante and Virgil move past the Furies and spy ". . .
an ample plain, / Full of distress and torment terrible."
    (IX, 110–111)

For flames between the sepulchers were scattered,

By which they so intensely heated were,

That iron more so asks not any art.

. . . from them issued forth such dire laments,

Sooth seemed they of the wretched and tormented.
    (IX, 118–120, 122–123)

This is where a variety of heretics are found—those
who founded heretical sects of every kind, together
with their disciples. None of the heretics are named,
but Dante summarizes, ". . . much / More than thou
thinkest laden are the tombs" (IX, 128-129).

The Schismatic

Epicurus

Dante peers closely at the tombs around, noting that their covers are lifted and no one seems to be keeping guard. Virgil tells him:

> . . . They all will be closed up
>> When from Jehosaphat they shall return
>> Here with the bodies they have left above.
> Their cemetery have upon this side
>> With Epicurus all his followers,
>> Who with the body mortal make the soul.
> (X, 10–15)

Jehosaphat is a biblical place, mentioned in Joel 3:2, a valley near Jerusalem that is said to be the site of the Last Judgment. There, all souls will claim their heavenly, or earthly, body as they are bound for heaven or hell.

To paraphrase Dante's lines about Epicurus, he and his followers have, by pursuing bodily pleasure, caused the soul to die right along with the body.

The Seventh Circle of Hell

CHAPTER ELEVEN

CIRCLE SEVEN
Pope Anastasius, Alexander the Great, Those of Self-Inflicted Violence

canto XI–XVII

HIS IS THE CIRCLE OF HELL RESIDENT to the most violent among us. Dante refers to them in the opening lines of canto XI as "a still more cruel throng" (3).

There are three layers to the souls condemned here, spread over several cantos. There are those who were violent to toward God, to themselves, and to others.

First found, somewhat puzzling, is **Pope Anastasius** (496–98), "Whom out of the right way Photinus drew," Dante says. This is usually understood to mean that this Pope was convinced to believe that Christ was only human, not divine. Dante places him in this lower, more violent, circle of hell, rather than with other heretics, probably because of the severity of the heresy and the apparent hiddenness and fraudulence of it.

> Violence can be done the Deity,
>> In heart denying and blaspheming Him. . . .
>> (XI, 46–47)

Minotaurs and centaurs are everywhere in the loathsome valley of canto XII, causing the pilgrim to exclaim:

> O blind cupidity, O wrath insane,
>> That spurs us onward so in our short life,
>> And in the eternal then so badly steeps us!
>> (XII, 49–51)

Alexander the Great

- Lived from 356–323 BC.

- A student of the philosopher Aristotle until he was 16.

- Recognized as one of the greatest military commanders in the history of warfare.

- Ruthless. Conquered most of the known world before he was 30.

With the great Macedonian emperor, Alexander, in sight, one of the centaurs preaches to all who can hear:

> . . . Tyrants are these,
> Who dealt in bloodshed and in pillaging.
> Here they lament their pitiless mischiefs. . . .
> (XII, 104–106)

Those of Self-Inflicted Violence

This category is one of the most difficult for us to accept in Dante's hell. The poet lived in a late medieval time when suicide was utterly shameful, often considered arrogant, and there was no understanding whatsoever of depression and other illnesses that can lead to such sad actions of self-inflicted harm. For these reasons, in canto XIII he views as worthy of eternal punishment those who have placed violent hands upon themselves—although it is clear that he also grieves for them, there.

CHAPTER TWELVE

CIRCLE EIGHT
Venedico Caccianemico, Pope Nicholas III, Emperor Constantine the Great

canto XVIII–XXXIII

HE PENULTIMATE SINNERS IN THE universe, found in these many later cantos, are those who committed sins of deception, seduction, and fraud.

Venedico Caccianemico

This first figure is another unfamiliar one to us, because he was a political opponent of Dante's in Florence in the years immediately preceding 1300. He was also, apparently, adept at swindling women. To Dante the pilgrim he confesses his "avaricious heart," and:

> While speaking in this manner, with his scourge
>> A demon smote him, and said: "Get thee gone,
>> Pander, there are no women here for coin."
>> (XVIII, 63, 64–66)

Venedico is an example of personal immorality spurred on by a headstrong desire for personal gain.

Pope Nicholas III

Next we see a pope. By this point, we are no longer shocked to see popes in Dante's hell! There are at least two, here, whom Dante calls out for the sin of simony—attempting to buy or sell a religious office.

Dante cries out against them:

> . . . O forlorn disciples,
> Ye who the things of God, which ought to be
> The brides of holiness, rapaciously
> For silver and for gold do prostitute.
> (XIX, 1–4)

And there we see Pope Nicholas III, who reigned as Holy Father from 1277–1280. He obstinately tells Dante:

> If who I am thou carest so much to know,
> That thou on that account hast crossed the bank,
> Know that I vested was with the great mantle;

And truly was I son of the She-bear,

> So eager to advance the cubs, that wealth

> Above, and here myself, I pocketed.

Beneath my head the others are dragged down

> Who have preceded me in simony.
> (XIX, 67–74)

In other words, he wasn't the first of popes to be found there, and he wouldn't be the last; Dante has Pope Nicholas tell us that Pope Boniface VIII, who was in the Petrine Chair at the time of this underworld journey (in AD 1300), would soon be coming, too!

Dante offers his reason for condemning to hell popes who pursued wealth for the Church (and sometimes themselves). He responds to Pope Nicholas with these words:

> I pray thee tell me now how great a treasure
> Our Lord demanded of Saint Peter first,

>> Before he put the keys into his keeping?

>> Truly he nothing asked but "Follow me."
>> (XIX, 90–93)

A rhetorical question, surely, which Dante answers for all.

Emperor Constantine the Great

Dante then turns to another famous figure from the early and medieval church: the Emperor Constantine, the first Roman emperor to embrace Christianity. Dante has troubled many people for 800 years with his placing of Constantine in the eighth circle of hell.

Why does he locate him there? Fraud. Let's allow Dante to say it first:

Ah, Constantine! of how much ill was mother,
    Not thy conversion, but that marriage-dower
    Which the first wealthy Father took from thee!
And while I sang to him such notes as these,
    Either that anger or that conscience stung him,
    He struggled violently with both his feet.
    (XIX, 115–120)

By "how much ill was mother" Dante means, "what bad seed was sown." And his reference to "that marriage-dower" is the metaphorical dowry that this first head of a Christian empire brought to marriage with the Church: the infamous "Donation of Constantine."

- The Donation of Constantine is the most famous forgery in the history of Christianity.

- It was a fake imperial decree that supposedly had Constantine giving control over Rome and the entire western half of the Roman Empire to the Pope.

- Constantine had nothing to do with writing the document.

- It was forged sometime during the eighth century.

- It was used by popes and others in the Church to justify many other "donations" of land and power over the centuries.

- "Why can't you be as generous to the Church as Emperor Constantine the Great once was?", they would say.

The Ninth Circle of Hell

CHAPTER THIRTEEN

CIRCLE NINE
Lucifer, Judas, Brutus and Cassius

cantos XXXII–XXXIV

INALLY, WE COME TO THE WORST SINNERS of all: those who betrayed. "[W]ith fear in verse I put it . . ." writes the pilgrim (XXXIV, 10), afraid to portray what he sees at this lowest point of all.

Lucifer

The sight of Lucifer, or Satan, is terrifying to Dante—
and to us! The evil angel had once been one of the
seraphim, and the description of his appearance in
hell's fury reminds us of that connection he had to
eternity:

The Emperor of the kingdom dolorous
  From his mid-breast forth issued from the ice;
  And better with a giant I compare
Than do the giants with those arms of his . . .
Were he as fair once, as he now is foul,
  And lifted up his brow against his Maker,
  Well may proceed from him all tribulation.
O, what a marvel it appeared to me,
  When I beheld three faces on his head!
  The one in front, and that vermillion was;
Two were the others, that were joined with this
  Above the middle part of either shoulder,
  And they were joined together at the crest . . .

Underneath each came forth two mighty wings,

Such as befitting were so great a bird;

Sails of the sea I never saw so large.
(XXXIV, 28–31, 34–43, 46–48)

- Lucifer is imagined to be constantly weeping out of six eyes at once.

- He is crunching the bodies of three sinners at a time in his teeth.

- This is going on—to each soul in his grasp—for eternity.

The first soul recognized by Virgil as in Lucifer's grasp, and pointed out to Dante, is Judas Iscariot.

The head of Judas is in the mouth of Lucifer, and his legs are flailing about.

Judas

- One of the original twelve disciples of Jesus.

The Judas Kiss

- The one who betrayed Jesus, turning him over to the Sanhedrin and Roman authorities in exchange for thirty silver coins.

- Then, according to Matthew 27:3–5:

  When Judas. . . saw that Jesus was condemned, he repented and brought back the thirty pieces of silver to the chief priests and the elders. He said, "I have sinned by betraying innocent blood." But they said, "What is that to us? See to it yourself." Throwing down the pieces of silver in the temple, he departed; and he went and hanged himself.

- Why is Judas the "great betrayer" in hell, since he seems to have recognized, confessed, and repented his sin? This mystery has been debated by Bible experts for centuries. But Jesus seems to have pronounced Judas's eternal destination, in a prayer to the Father, even before he went to the cross:

Holy Father, protect them in your name that you have given me, so that they may be one, as we are one. While I was with them, I protected them in your name that you have given me. I guarded them, and not one of them was lost except the one destined to be lost, so that the scripture might be fulfilled. (John 17:11–12)

Brutus and Cassius

Next are Brutus and Cassius, also head downward in Lucifer's jaws forever.

"See how he writhes himself, and speaks no word," explains Virgil to Dante, about Brutus. "And the other, who so stalwart seems, is Cassius."
(XXXIV, 66–67)

Who are these Brutus and Cassius, who deserve to be there with Satan and Judas at the bottom of hell?

- Brutus and Cassius were the assassins of the Roman Emperor Julius Caesar.
- Marcus Junius Brutus lived from 85–42 BC.

- He was a Roman politician and co-leader with Cassius of eight Roman senators who stabbed Julius Caesar to death on March 15, 44 BC.

- Gaius Cassius Longinus also lived from 85–42 BC.

- He was an Epicurean philosopher, in addition to being a politician.

- The two men fought together in a final battle for Rome in October 42 BC. Cassius died in that battle, while Brutus retreated to the woods—where he killed himself.

Return to the Fair World

Conclusion

IRGIL AND THE PILGRIM, DANTE, end their journey after this most horrible vision in the ninth and bottommost circle of hell. The pilgrim tells how they then make their way back into the sunshine of life once again:

A place there is below, from Beelzebub
    As far receding as the tomb extends,
      Which not by sight is known, but by the sound

Rebeholding the Stars

Of a small rivulet, that there descendeth

Through chasm within the stone, which it has
gnawed

With course that winds about and slightly falls.

The Guide and I into that hidden road

Now entered, to return to the bright world;

And without care of having any rest

We mounted up, he first and I the second,

Till I beheld through a round aperture

Some of those beauteous things which Heaven
doth bear;

Thence we came forth to rebehold the stars.

(XXXIV, 127–139)

In Dante's era, that eternal place of damnation was thought to lie, as below "a small rivulet," down in the bowels of the earth itself. Walking about on earth was supposed to be a constant reminder of what lies below our feet.

So what is the "takeaway" from reading Dante's *Inferno?* That is the question that, by now, we want answered. All of these faces in such an awful crowd—what relevance do they have for our lives, today?

Dante might say: Learn from the mistakes of those who have gone before you. Guard your heart. Be a follower of Christ, and not bedeviled by the evil one. The meaning of this *Inferno* surely lies, for us, in this advice.

It is also surely metaphorical. We have our own "hells" to traverse. And our sins put us in a kind of hell. St. Augustine recognized this in one of the more quoted passages from his great memoir, *The Confessions*:

> And lo, there was I received by the scourge of bodily sickness, and I was going down to Hell, carrying all the sins which I had committed, both against Thee, and myself, and others, many and grievous, over and above that bond of original sin, whereby we all die in Adam. . . . So true, then, was the

death of my soul, as that of His flesh seemed to me false; and how true the death of His body, so false was the life of my soul.

Augustine is talking about nothing less than his own conversion, a process by which he died to himself and, by so doing, discovered himself anew in God. We often need a kind of "hell" in order to find our way.

For Dante, that kind of understanding comes only through the journeying itself, through seeing and experiencing the sort of suffering that he has seen and experienced. Then, the poet said, he was finally able to know how to live rightly.

Note

1. Peter S. Hawkins, *Dante's Testaments: Essays in Scriptural Imagination*; Stanford, CA: Stanford University Press, 1999; 7.

About Paraclete Press

Who We Are

Paraclete Press is a publisher of books, recordings, and DVDs on Christian spirituality. Our publishing represents a full expression of Christian belief and practice—from Catholic to Evangelical, from Protestant to Orthodox.

We are the publishing arm of the Community of Jesus, an ecumenical monastic community in the Benedictine tradition. As such, we are uniquely positioned in the marketplace without connection to a large corporation and with informal relationships to many branches and denominations of faith.

What We Are Doing

Books • Paraclete publishes books that show the richness and depth of what it means to be Christian. Although Benedictine spirituality is at the heart of all that we do, we publish books that reflect the Christian experience across many cultures, time periods, and houses of worship. We publish books that nourish the vibrant life of the church and its people—books about spiritual practice, formation, history, ideas, and customs.

We have several different series, including the best-selling Paraclete Essentials and Paraclete Giants series of classic texts in contemporary English; A Voice from the

Monastery—men and women monastics writing about living a spiritual life today; award-winning poetry; best-selling gift books for children on the occasions of baptism and first communion; and the Active Prayer Series that brings creativity and liveliness to any life of prayer.

Recordings • From Gregorian chant to contemporary American choral works, our music recordings celebrate sacred choral music through the centuries. Paraclete distributes the recordings of the internationally acclaimed choir Gloriæ Dei Cantores, praised for their "rapt and fathomless spiritual intensity" by *American Record Guide*, and the Gloriæ Dei Cantores Schola, which specializes in the study and performance of Gregorian chant. Paraclete is also the exclusive North American distributor of the recordings of the Monastic Choir of St. Peter's Abbey in Solesmes, France, long considered to be a leading authority on Gregorian chant.

Videos • Our videos offer spiritual help, healing, and biblical guidance for life issues: grief and loss, marriage, forgiveness, anger management, facing death, and spiritual formation.

Learn more about us at our website: www.paracletepress.com, or call us toll-free at 1-800-451-5006.

SCAN
TO
READ
MORE

You may also be interested in ...

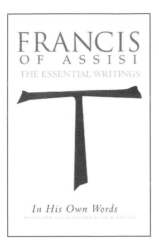

Francis of Assisi in His Own Words

Translated and annotated by Jon M. Sweeney

ISBN: 978-1-61261-069-6 $14.99 Paperback

BIOGRAPHIES OF ST. FRANCIS will only take you so far. To truly understand him, read his own writings. Sweeney has compiled all of the ones that we are most certain come from Francis himself, including his first Rule of life and many others. An introduction and explanatory notes throughout the book help to put the writings into historical and theological context.

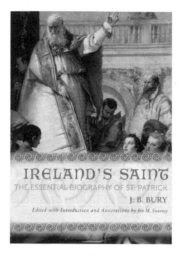

Ireland's Saint
J. B. Bury

ISBN: 978-1-61261-333-8 $9.99 Paperback

EXPLORE PATRICK'S PLACE IN HISTORY. This 21st-century edition includes notes from other notable biographers, mystics, historians, and storytellers of Ireland and is an ideal place to begin any exploration of this much loved but little-known saint.

Available from most booksellers or through Paraclete Press: www.paracletepress.com; 1-800-451-5006.
Try your local bookstore first.